SCHOLASTIC

ACTIVE™ Grammar

Practice Book 1

AF530511

Rosemary Allen

Name ______________________________

Class ______________________________

© 2012 Scholastic Education International (Singapore) Private Limited
A division of Scholastic Inc.

Previously published as Grammar Skills 1 by Learners Publishing Pte Ltd.

All rights reserved. No part of this publication may be reproduced in whole or in part, or stored in a retrieval system, or transmitted in any form or by any means, electronic, mechanical, photocopying, recording, or otherwise without the written permission of the publisher.

First edition 2012
Reprinted 2012, 2013 (thrice), 2014 (thrice), 2015 (twice), 2016, 2017, 2018, 2019, 2020, 2022, 2024, 2025, 2026

ISBN 978-81-8477-746-8

CONTENTS

© 2012 Scholastic Education International (S) Pte Ltd ISBN 978-81-8477-746-8

To Teachers and Parents

The study of English grammar in schools is changing as educators become increasingly aware of the important role context plays in language learning. The functional use of grammar has become a feature of English syllabuses around the world.

Active Grammar Practice Books have been written specifically to provide students with valuable links between basic, traditional grammatical concepts and the functional contexts in which they are used. The activities represent a blend of traditional and functional approaches to describe how texts 'work' in real-life situations and why certain grammatical choices are considered appropriate. Traditional grammar serves to provide students with the special terminology needed to talk about grammar, while functional grammar is intended to improve communicative competence by showing students how grammar works in the context of different text types.

The exercises in this book give students systematic guidance in developing an understanding of grammatical concepts. Throughout the books there are panel notes that give hints for correct usage and highlight exceptions to grammar rules, as well as provide simple non-technical definitions to help students understand the exercises. Many of the exercises incorporate learner-centred activities that include completing rhymes and short stories, solving riddles and puzzles, doing word searches and seeing 'language-in-action'. At the same time, the activities provide teachers with a range of techniques to use, techniques that have proven highly successful with both native and non-native speakers of English. The exercises are graded, but include challenging ones to motivate as well as interest the students.

It is hoped that teachers will find this series a valuable tool in their teaching programme, one that will provide young learners with a fascinating journey into the world of English language and a sound knowledge of how it works.

© 2012 Scholastic Education International (S) Pte Ltd ISBN 978-81-8477-746-8

1 The Alphabet

Grammar Help

There are **26 letters** in the English **alphabet**.
The letters of the alphabet always have the same order.
This order is called **alphabetical order**.

A ***This shop is in a mess. Help the florist rearrange the flowers. Put the words for them in alphabetical order.***

1.

2.

3.

4.

5.

6.

7.

© 2012 Scholastic Education International (S) Pte Ltd ISBN 978-81-8477-746-8

Grammar Help

The letters **a**, **e**, **i**, **o** and **u** are called **vowels**.

All the other letters are called **consonants**.

B ***Look at the Grammar Help. Then do the following.***

1. Circle the vowels.

a	b	c	d	e	f	g
h	i	j	k	l	m	n
o	p	q	r	s	t	u
v	w	x	y	z		

There are ______ vowels in the alphabet.

2. Write the consonants.

____

____

____

There are ______ consonants in the alphabet.

C ***All these words have vowels in them. Write the vowels in the blanks.***

1. alphabet ____ ____ ____
2. umbrella ____ ____ ____
3. ostrich ____ ____
4. lollipop ____ ____ ____
5. consonant ____ ____ ____
6. pumpkin ____ ____

© 2012 Scholastic Education International (S) Pte Ltd ISBN 978-81-8477-746-8

D *For each row, make as many words as you can with the letters on the left and using different vowels. The first row has been done as an example.*

1. b ☐ d bad ____ bed ____ bid ____ bud ____
2. f ☐ n ____ ____ ____ ____
3. p ☐ n ____ ____ ____ ____
4. d ☐ g ____ ____ ____ ____
5. n ☐ t ____ ____ ____ ____
6. m ☐ p ____ ____ ____ ____
7. l ☐ g ____ ____ ____ ____
8. c ☐ t ____ ____ ____ ____

E *How many words can you make with the following letters? Begin each word with the consonant* **s** *.*

© 2012 Scholastic Education International (S) Pte Ltd ISBN 978-81-8477-746-8

2 Capital Letters and Small Letters

Grammar Help

Words that name things are called **nouns**. Nouns also name people, animals and places.

A ***This picture shows the order of the letters on your computer keyboard. They are all capital letters.***

Make a keyboard using small letters. Use the same order as the keyboard above.

B ***Draw a line to match each object with the noun for it.***

football	apple	calendar	doll

© 2012 Scholastic Education International (S) Pte Ltd ISBN 978-81-8477-746-8

C *Look at the picture.*

1. Colour the capital letters red and the small letters blue.

2. Name each thing that has a small letter next to it.
   The noun begins with the small letter.

b ____________ **k** ____________ **n** ____________ **d** ____________

f ____________ **t** ____________ **g** ____________ **c** ____________

© 2012 Scholastic Education International (S) Pte Ltd ISBN 978-81-8477-746-8

Grammar Help

A person's **special name** always begins with a **capital letter**.

3. Give a name to each child in the picture.
   The name must start with the letter on his or her T-shirt.

A ____________ S ____________ T ____________

H ____________ K ____________ M ____________

4. Find eight names of people in the word-search box below.
   Write the names in the name tags.
   Be sure to start each name with a capital letter.

(a)

(b)

(c)

(d)

j	a	m	e	s	p
f	t	o	m	s	o
d	i	a	n	a	m
p	b	i	l	l	a
a	o	a	r	l	r
t	b	s	u	y	k

(e)

(f)

(g)

(h)

© 2012 Scholastic Education International (S) Pte Ltd ISBN 978-81-8477-746-8

Grammar Help

The **special name** of a person, animal, place or thing usually begins with a capital letter for each word in the name.

D ***Fill in the names. Begin each word of each name with a capital letter.***

1. My friend's name is ______________________________.
2. My favourite book is ______________________________.
3. My favourite TV show is ______________________________.
4. My school is in ______________________________.
5. My country is ______________________________.

E ***The address on the small envelope is in small letters. Rewrite the address correctly, using capital letters where necessary.***

© 2012 Scholastic Education International (S) Pte Ltd ISBN 978-81-8477-746-8

3 a, an, the

A ***Read the story and underline each a, an and the.***

The Gingerbread Boy

Once there was an old man and an old woman. They lived in a little house on the top of a hill. They felt lonely.

One day, the old woman had an idea. She would make a boy to keep them company. So she mixed an egg and some ginger powder with a large bowl of flour. She made the shape of a little boy with the dough. Then she put the 'boy' in the oven to bake.

After an hour, the old woman opened the oven door to take the boy out. To her surprise, the Gingerbread Boy jumped up and ran out of the house and down the hill. Very sadly, the old woman watched him run away.

© 2012 Scholastic Education International (S) Pte Ltd ISBN 978-81-8477-746-8

B ***What do you see in this picture?***
Put a or an before the word in each box.
Then read each phrase aloud with the words in the bubble.

© 2012 Scholastic Education International (S) Pte Ltd ISBN 978-81-8477-746-8

C *Fill in each blank with **a** or **an**.*

1. _____ egg sleeping in _____ basket

2. _____ octopus hiding under _____ rock

3. _____ fox riding on _____ elephant

4. _____ bear flying _____ aeroplane

5. _____ monkey holding _____ umbrella

6. _____ owl working at _____ computer

© 2012 Scholastic Education International (S) Pte Ltd ISBI

D *Fill in each blank in each story with a, an or the.*

The Three Billy Goats Gruff

I like _____ story of _____ Three Billy Goats Gruff.

_____ three goats wanted to eat green grass.

But to get to _____ green grass they had to cross _____ bridge.

Under _____ bridge lived _____ angry troll.

He didn't want _____ goats to cross over _____ bridge.

The Selfish Giant

Once there was _____ large and beautiful garden.

In _____ garden there lived _____ selfish giant.

_____ giant did not want anyone to play in _____

garden, so he built _____ strong wall around it.

Jack and the Beanstalk

I like _____ story of Jack and _____ beanstalk.

Jack got some magic beans from _____ old man.

He planted _____ beans and they grew up to _____ clouds.

Jack climbed up and stole _____ hen from _____ giant

because he saw it lay _____ egg of gold.

© 2012 Scholastic Education International (S) Pte Ltd ISBN 978-81-8477-746-8

4 Common Nouns

Grammar Help

Common nouns are names of ordinary things you see around you.

A ***Look at each picture. Fill in the blank in the sentence with a common noun.***

1. 

Look carefully before you cross the ______________.

2. 

The ______________ opened suddenly.

3. 

Miss Lee is reading her pupils a ______________.

4. 

My uncle is a ______________.

5. 

The ______________ is very smart.

6. 

Dad and I are watching ______________.

7. 

Mr Lang is our bus ______________.

8. 

Kathy plays the ______________.

© 2012 Scholastic Education International (S) Pte Ltd ISBN 978-81-8477-746-8

B ***Look at this picture. Fill in the blanks below with the names of things, creatures and people you see.***

1. Four common nouns that begin with the letter **f**.

    (a) ____________ (c) ____________

    (b) ____________ (d) ____________

2. Four common nouns that begin with the letter **s**.

    (a) ____________ (c) ____________

    (b) ____________ (d) ____________

3. Four common nouns that begin with the letter **b**.

    (a) ____________ (c) ____________

    (b) ____________ (d) ____________

© 2012 Scholastic Education International (S) Pte Ltd ISBN 978-81-8477-746-8

4. The names of four creatures.

(a) ____________________ (c) ____________________

(b) ____________________ (d) ____________________

5. Four common nouns that refer to people.

(a) ____________________ (c) ____________________

(b) ____________________ (d) ____________________

6. The names of four other things you see in the park.

(a) ____________________ (c) ____________________

(b) ____________________ (d) ____________________

© 2012 Scholastic Education International (S) Pte Ltd ISBN 978-81-8477-746-8

C Complete the puzzle with common nouns. Use the picture clues to help you.

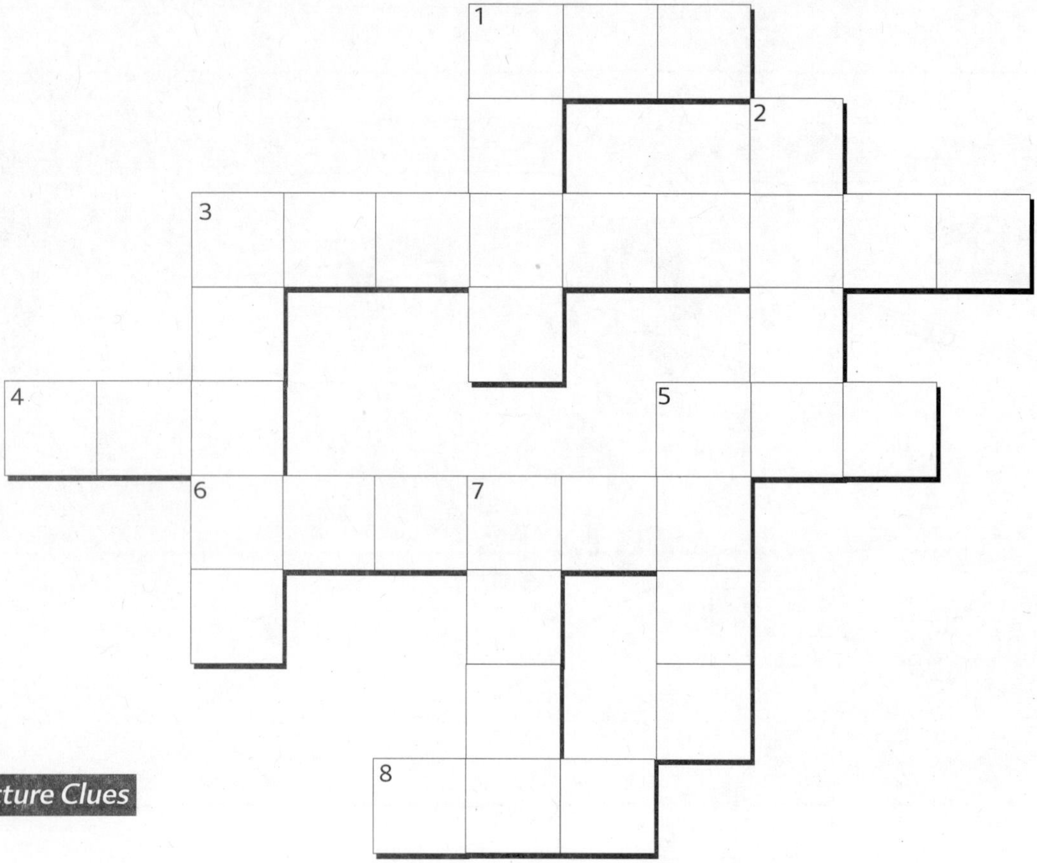

Picture Clues

Across

1 

3 

4 

5 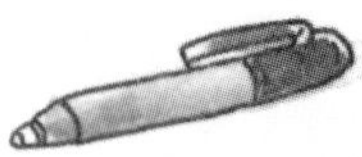

6 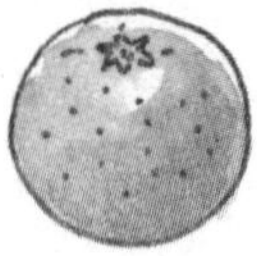

8 

Down

1 

2 

3 

5 

7 

© 2012 Scholastic Education International (S) Pte Ltd ISBN 978-81-8477-746-8

5 Proper Nouns

Grammar Help

Proper nouns are special names of people, countries, cities, rivers, mountains, streets, places, buildings, months and days.

A *Look at this picture of a street corner.*

1. Write the names of two banks.

   (a) ______________________ (b) ______________________

2. Write the names of four special buildings.

   (a) ______________________ (c) ______________________

   (b) ______________________ (d) ______________________

3. Write the names of three streets or roads.

   (a) ______________________ (c) ______________________

   (b) ______________________

4. Each proper noun begins with a __________ letter.

© 2012 Scholastic Education International (S) Pte Ltd ISBN 978-81-8477-746-8

B ***Write the days of the week in the correct order in the calendar. Then complete the following sentences with the correct words.***

Wednesday	Saturday	Monday
Friday	Tuesday	Thursday

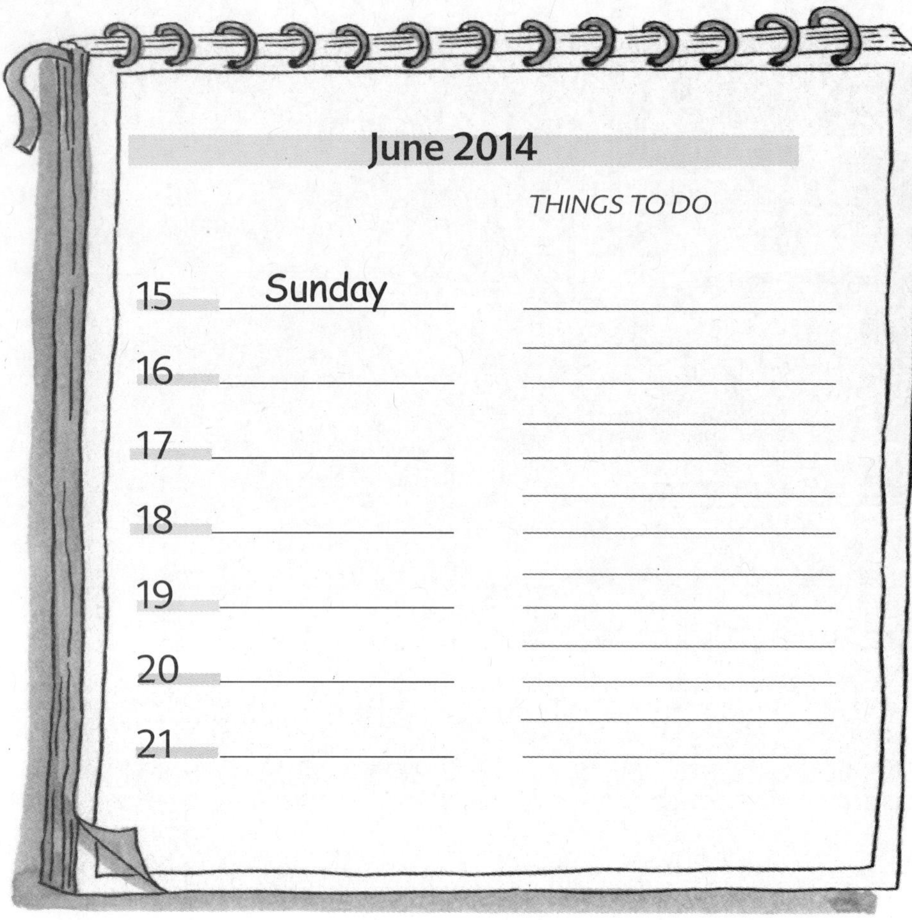

1. The first day of the week is ____________.
2. The fifth day of the week is ____________.
3. Days of the week are ____________ nouns.
4. The proper nouns begin with ____________ letters.

© 2012 Scholastic Education International (S) Pte Ltd ISBN 978-81-8477-746-8

C ***Below are the twelve pages of a calendar. Fill in the months in the correct order. The first month is filled in for you.***

December	October
November	June
August	September
July	January
March	February
May	April

© 2012 Scholastic Education International (S) Pte Ltd ISBN 978-81-8477-746-8

D ***Underline the proper nouns in the sentences. Then write the proper nouns in the chart.***

1. "The Golden Goose" is an interesting storybook.
2. My friend Alice is the top girl in my class.
3. Have you read the story of Pinocchio?
4. James is a student at Winton Primary School.
5. Tourists like to go to King's Road to shop.
6. I saw the movie "The Lion King" on Saturday.
7. We celebrate Mother's Day next month.
8. Her birthday falls on Christmas Day.
9. Dr Lee works in York Hospital.
10. We are going to the National Zoo.

People	Places

Books and Movies	Special Days

© 2012 Scholastic Education International (S) Pte Ltd ISBN 978-81-8477-746-8

6 Singular and Plural Nouns

Grammar Help

Singular means **one**. **Plural** means **more than one**.

Plural nouns may end with the letter **s**.

A ***Look at this picture of a boy. Then complete the sentences with the correct singular or plural nouns.***

body, nose, head, chest, face, tongue, mouth

legs, arms, ears, eyes, hands, fingers, knees, toes

1. The boy has one ____________, one ____________, one ____________, one ____________, one ____________, one ____________ and one ____________.
2. He has two ____________, two ____________, two ____________, two ____________, two ____________ and two ____________.
3. He has ten ____________ and ten ____________.

© 2012 Scholastic Education International (S) Pte Ltd ISBN 978-81-8477-746-8

B Put each noun in the correct group.

flower	books	children	fan
ant	violin	foxes	kites
dishes	crab	stars	egg
song	chairs	garden	trains

Singular Nouns	Plural Nouns
1. ______	1. ______
2. ______	2. ______
3. ______	3. ______
4. ______	4. ______
5. ______	5. ______
6. ______	6. ______
7. ______	7. ______
8. ______	8. ______

© 2012 Scholastic Education International (S) Pte Ltd ISBN 978-81-8477-746-8

Grammar Help

For singular nouns that end in **s**, **x**, **ch** or **sh**, you add **-es** to form the plurals.

C

All these nouns are singular.
Add -s or -es to the nouns to make them plural.

1. fox ______________________

2. toothbrush ______________________

3. camel ______________________

4. clown ______________________

5. glass ______________________

6. dentist ______________________

7. tree ______________________

8. peach ______________________

9. bench ______________________

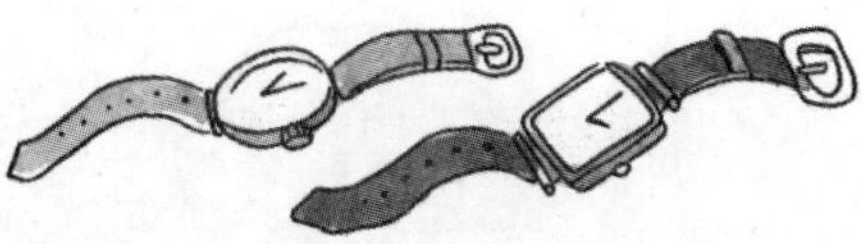

10. watch ______________________

© 2012 Scholastic Education International (S) Pte Ltd ISBN 978-81-8477-746-8

Grammar Help

When a singular noun ends in **y**, you change the **y** to **i** and add **-es** to make it plural. But for some nouns, you just add **-s** to make them plural.

Examples: story – stor**ies** day – day**s**

D *Make these singular nouns that end in* **y** *plural.*

1. lady ____________________

6. fairy ____________________

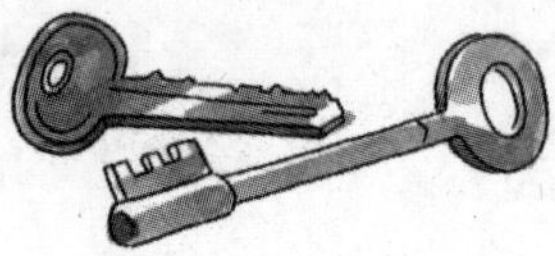

2. key ____________________

7. cherry ____________________

3. toy ____________________

8. housefly ____________________

4. donkey ____________________

9. puppy ____________________

5. baby ____________________

10. boy ____________________

© 2012 Scholastic Education International (S) Pte Ltd ISBN 978-81-8477-746-8

7 Countable and Uncountable Nouns

Grammar Help

Countable nouns are for things that can be counted; **uncountable nouns** are for things that cannot be counted.
You cannot make an **uncountable noun** plural.

A ***Sue is helping her mother to make some scones. Here are the words for the utensils and ingredients they are using. Put each noun in the correct group below.***

Utensils :	bowl	sieve	teaspoon	wooden spoon
	knife	whisk	tray	
Ingredients :	flour	salt	sugar	baking powder
	egg	milk	butter	

Countable Nouns	Uncountable Nouns
______________	______________
______________	______________
______________	______________
______________	______________
______________	______________
______________	______________
______________	______________
______________	______________

© 2012 Scholastic Education International (S) Pte Ltd ISBN 978-81-8477-746-8

B ***Read what Frog and Rabbit say. Then write the nouns that belong to their lists.***

book	grass	gold	snow	flower
milk	water	table	zoo	money
air	car	rain	hen	door
shoe	sand	cake	oil	nut

Countable Nouns	Uncountable Nouns
______________	______________
______________	______________
______________	______________
______________	______________
______________	______________
______________	______________
______________	______________
______________	______________
______________	______________
______________	______________

© 2012 Scholastic Education International (S) Pte Ltd ISBN 978-81-8477-746-8

C ***Look at the words in bold print in the sentences. Are they countable nouns or uncountable nouns? Write C for countable nouns and UC for uncountable nouns on the lines.***

__________ 1. There's a **nest** in the tree.

__________ 2. Cheese is made from **milk**.

__________ 3. A square has four **sides**.

__________ 4. I took a ride in his **car**.

__________ 5. The children are flying **kites**.

__________ 6. Some **guests** have arrived.

__________ 7. Wipe the **mud** off the floor.

__________ 8. There is some **dirt** on my shirt.

__________ 9. Does your **dog** have a licence?

__________ 10. He has enough **paint** for all the walls of the house.

© 2012 Scholastic Education International (S) Pte Ltd ISBN 978-81-8477-746-8

D ***Read the story carefully.***
Then put each word in bold in the correct group below.

The Rescue

High up in a **tree** there sat a mother **bird** in her **nest**. The nest was made of **wool, sticks, mud, moss** and **leaves**. Suddenly, the **wind** began to blow strongly. It moved the mother bird from side to side in the nest. The three **eggs** under her were also tossed about. All at once, one of the eggs fell out of the nest. The egg fell into the **lake** below the tree branch. The mother bird began to chirp loudly for **help**. A **boy** who was swimming in the lake picked up the egg. He climbed up the tree and put the egg back in the nest. The mother bird was happy again.

Countable Nouns	Uncountable Nouns
____________	____________
____________	____________
____________	____________
____________	____________
____________	____________
____________	____________
____________	____________
____________	____________

© 2012 Scholastic Education International (S) Pte Ltd ISBN 978-81-8477-746-8

8 Masculine and Feminine Nouns

Grammar Help

Masculine gender refers to males. **Feminine gender** refers to females.

A *Write the masculine noun for each word.*

Feminine	Masculine
1. mother	______________
2. grandmother	______________
3. niece	______________
4. headmistress	______________
5. girlfriend	______________
6. empress	______________
7. hen	______________
8. cow	______________
9. lioness	______________
10. tigress	______________

© 2012 Scholastic Education International (S) Pte Ltd ISBN 978-81-8477-746-8

B *Write the correct feminine noun for the caption of each photograph.*

1. My father and ____________

2. My uncle and ____________

3. A man and a ____________

4. A waiter and a ____________

5. My brother and ____________

6. Their son and ____________

7. A prince and a ____________

8. A bridegroom and a ____________

© 2012 Scholastic Education International (S) Pte Ltd ISBN 978-81-8477-746-8

C ***Look at the animal families on this page.***
Write M for each masculine noun and F for each feminine noun.
Write M/F if the noun is not masculine or feminine.

hen

rooster

chick

nanny goat

billy goat

kid

cow

bull

calf

lion

cub

lioness

© 2012 Scholastic Education International (S) Pte Ltd ISBN 978-81-8477-746-8

D *Find five masculine nouns and five feminine nouns in the word-search box. Circle them.*

B	O	Y	D	B	E	T	K
A	K	C	O	C	K	I	J
A	I	F	G	H	E	G	M
Y	N	Z	W	E	X	R	S
T	G	M	A	N	U	E	R
M	O	T	H	E	R	S	S
E	M	P	R	E	S	S	L
J	K	M	A	I	D	Q	U

E *Change the masculine nouns to feminine nouns.*

1. That **boy** (____________) is my **nephew** (____________).
2. The **waiter** (____________) served the **King** (____________).
3. The **lion** (____________) hunted the **bull** (____________).
4. That **man** (____________) is a famous **actor** (____________).
5. The **bridegroom** (____________) is my **uncle** (____________).

© 2012 Scholastic Education International (S) Pte Ltd ISBN 978-81-8477-746-8

9 Pronouns

Grammar Help

You do not always have to repeat proper nouns or common nouns.
You can use **pronouns** instead.

A Use the correct pronouns to complete the sentences.

she	**it**
they	**he**

1. This is Jack.

   ______ likes football.

2. This is Lisa.

   ______ likes roller skating.

3. This is a bus.

   ______ travels along Hill Road.

4. This is the Chen family.

   ______ catch the bus to town.

© 2012 Scholastic Education International (S) Pte Ltd ISBN 978-81-8477-746-8

B Read this story about three bears.

Once upon a time there were three bears. They lived in a cottage in the forest.

First there was Father Bear. He was a great big bear. Then there was Mother Bear. She was a medium-sized bear. And then there was Baby Bear. He was a tiny little bear.

One morning Mother Bear made porridge as usual and poured it into three bowls. But as the porridge was too hot to eat, Mother Bear, Father Bear and Baby Bear left their bowls to cool and went for a walk.

1. Underline the **pronouns** in the story.
2. What does the word **it** refer to in the story? ____________________
3. Here are pictures of the three bears. Write the correct **pronouns** below their names.

Father Bear

____

Mother Bear

____

Baby Bear

____

The Bear Family

____

© 2012 Scholastic Education International (S) Pte Ltd ISBN 978-81-8477-746-8

C *Answer the questions. Use these pronouns in your answers.*

She	It	They	He	We	I

1. What school do you go to?

____

2. Who are your friends? (Name two of them.)

____

3. When is your birthday?

____

4. What do you and your friends like to do together?

____

5. What food does your father like?

____

6. What food does your mother like?

____

© 2012 Scholastic Education International (S) Pte Ltd ISBN 978-81-8477-746-8

D ***Complete this story, using the pronouns correctly. You may use some of the pronouns more than once.***

it	I	me
them	him	her
you	they	we

The Little Red Hen

One day, the Little Red Hen found some corn. (1) She met a duck and said to (2) ________, "Will (3) ________ help (4) ________ plant the corn?" The duck said, "No!"

The Little Red Hen met a rooster. (5) ________ asked (6) ________, "Will (7) ________ help (8) ________ plant my corn?" The rooster said, "No!"

Then the Little Red Hen met a goose and a gander and she asked (9) ________ if (10) ________ would help (11) ________ plant the corn. (12) ________ said, "No!"

The Little Red Hen told (13) ________, "Then (14) ________ will plant (15) ________ myself. My chicks and (16) ________ will eat the corn. (17) ________ will not share (18) ________ with (19) ________ because (20) ________ didn't help."

© 2012 Scholastic Education International (S) Pte Ltd ISBN 978-81-8477-746-8

10 this, that, these, those

Grammar Help

You use **this** when you talk about something close by.
You use **that** when you talk about some other thing further away.

A *Look at each picture. Complete what the person says using This is or That is.*

1.

2.

3.

4.

5.

6.

7.

8.

© 2012 Scholastic Education International (S) Pte Ltd ISBN 978-81-8477-746-8

Grammar Help

You use **these** when you talk about more than one thing close by.
You use **those** when you talk about more than one thing further away.

B *Look at each picture. Complete the sentence with **these** or **those**.*

1. I don't want __________ shoes.

2. Give me __________ books.

3. __________ are apartments.

4. __________ are houses.

5. __________ are donkeys.

6. __________ are horses.

7. __________ are my roller skates.

8. __________ are bats.

© 2012 Scholastic Education International (S) Pte Ltd ISBN 978-81-8477-746-8

C *Complete each question with **this, that, these** or **those.***

1. Whose socks are __________?

2. Whose racket is __________?

3. What bird is __________?

4. What flowers are __________?

5. What building is __________?

6. What is __________?

7. Whose books are __________?

8. Whose watch is __________?

9. Whose bags are __________?

10. What place is __________?

© 2012 Scholastic Education International (S) Pte Ltd ISBN 978-81-8477-746-8

D *Fill in each blank with* ***this, that, these*** *or* ***those.***

Miss Lee is showing a new boy around the school.

Miss Lee: I hope you like our school. (1) ____________ is the Computer Room and (2) ____________ is the Library over there.

Student: Can we use the computers?

Miss Lee: You can use (3) ____________ computers here, but (4) ____________ computers over there are only for the older students.

Student: Where do Year One students sit?

Miss Lee: Right here! (5) ____________ section is for you and other Year One students. See the seats over there?

(6) ____________ section is for Year Three students.

Student: Oh, so (7) ____________ seats here are for Year One students and (8) ____________ seats are for the students in Year Three.

Miss Lee: Yes. Now, let us go back to class so you can meet your classmates.

© 2012 Scholastic Education International (S) Pte Ltd ISBN 978-81-8477-746-8

11 Adjectives

A *This is the back cover of a children's science book. Read what it tells you about the book.*

New Age Science for Children

This colourful book has been specially written for children between the ages of six and nine. It contains interesting information about 1000 everyday things. All the explanations are given in clear, simple language, with lots of colourful drawings and photographs.

The book serves as a useful companion for young children. It provides answers to the many questions that they often ask.

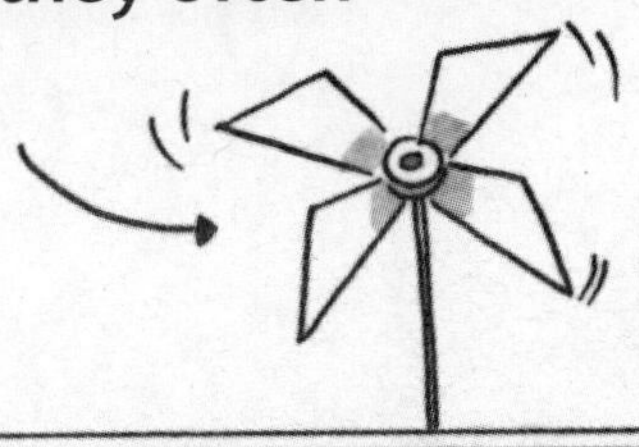

LEARNERS PUBLISHING

Here are some nouns used in the text.
Write the adjective that describes each noun.

1. ______________ children
2. ______________ book
3. ______________ information
4. ______________ things
5. ______________ language
6. ______________ drawings

© 2012 Scholastic Education International (S) Pte Ltd ISBN 978-81-8477-746-8

B Use a suitable adjective to describe each noun.

1. house

2. man

3. flowers

4. building

5. day

difficult

dirty

beautiful

strong

happy

dry

old

large

tall

cold

6. boy

7. land

8. sums

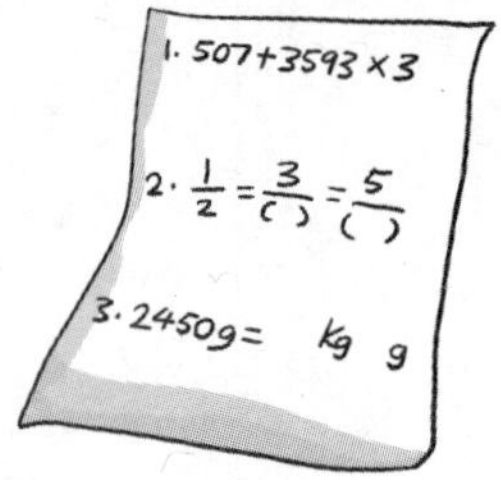

9. ship

10. children

© 2012 Scholastic Education International (S) Pte Ltd ISBN 978-81-8477-746-8

C ***Underline the adjective in each sentence. Then write a different adjective in the space provided. See the example given.***

Example

Sally has a <u>pretty</u> doll. big

1. She is a young lady. ____________________
2. Harry's dog has a short tail. ____________________
3. They all sat at the round table. ____________________
4. The girl is wearing a red dress. ____________________
5. There is an empty jug on the tray. ____________________
6. He is driving a small car. ____________________
7. That is a good idea. ____________________
8. This is an easy sum. ____________________
9. Joe is a clever boy. ____________________
10. It is a rainy day. ____________________

© 2012 Scholastic Education International (S) Pte Ltd ISBN 978-81-8477-746-8

Grammar Help

Words that have the same, or are similar in, meaning are called **synonyms**.

D *Choose the most suitable synonym for each word in the left column.*

1. happy ____________________
2. small ____________________
3. big ____________________
4. simple ____________________
5. rich ____________________
6. quiet ____________________
7. difficult ____________________
8. tidy ____________________
9. beautiful ____________________
10. bad ____________________

easy
cheerful
neat
silent
pretty
little
wealthy
hard
wicked
large

© 2012 Scholastic Education International (S) Pte Ltd ISBN 978-81-8477-746-8

12 Possessive Adjectives

Grammar Help

Some **adjectives** are used to show that the objects they describe belong to someone.
They are called **possessive adjectives** or **possessive determiners**.

A ***Continue reading the story about the three bears. Underline all the possessive adjectives in the story.***

The Three Bears

After a long walk, the three bears returned to their cottage. They were surprised to find someone had been there.

"Somebody has been eating my porridge!" cried Father Bear.

"Somebody has been eating your porridge, too!" Father Bear pointed at Mother Bear's porridge. Mother Bear looked at her porridge.

"Look! Somebody has been eating his porridge!" Father Bear said to Mother Bear, pointing at Baby Bear's porridge.

"Oh! Somebody has been eating our porridge!" the three bears complained.

© 2012 Scholastic Education International (S) Pte Ltd ISBN 978-81-8477-746-8

B ***Use the given possessive adjectives to complete the sentences. You have to use one of them twice.***

her	my	his	our	your	its	their

1. I can't come with you. I have to finish __________ homework.
2. You must finish __________ homework, too.
3. Has John finished __________ homework yet?
4. No, he has been to see __________ grandmother.
5. She has hurt __________ leg.
6. All our friends have finished __________ homework.
7. We must finish __________ homework, too.
8. I'll do it as soon as I've put this jigsaw back in __________ box.

© 2012 Scholastic Education International (S) Pte Ltd ISBN 978-81-8477-746-8

C ***Fill in the blanks with the correct possessive adjectives. You have to use some of them more than once.***

her	my	his	our	your	its	their

1. Joe and __________ friends are playing chess. They play chess every afternoon.
2. Some rich people like to show off __________ wealth. They wear a lot of jewellery.
3. This book has lost __________ cover. We must give it a new cover.
4. Alice hurt __________ arm in the accident. She is now at the doctor's clinic.
5. Children, check __________ answers carefully.
6. We are cheering __________ team on.
7. I have a dog. This is __________ dog.

8. Janet always makes __________ own bed. She does this when she gets up in the morning.
9. The trees have shed __________ leaves. They are quite bare now.

10. The man has forgotten to bring __________ passport. He has to go home to fetch it.

© 2012 Scholastic Education International (S) Pte Ltd ISBN 978-81-8477-746-8

D *Look at each picture. Use **my, your, his, her, its, our** or **their** to complete the sentence on the picture.*

1. Ann is playing __________ violin.

2. The hen is sitting on __________ eggs.

3. I am cutting __________ birthday cake.

4. You must eat __________ lunch before it gets cold.

5. John fell and broke __________ ankle.

6. We always wash __________ hands before dinner.

7. They hang up __________ clothes in the wardrobe.

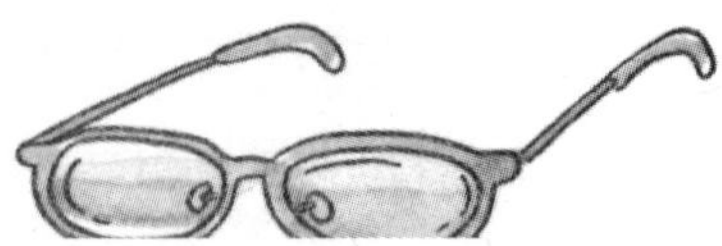

8. Grandma is looking for __________ glasses.

© 2012 Scholastic Education International (S) Pte Ltd ISBN 978-81-8477-746-8

13 Prepositions

Grammar Help

Prepositions are words that tell you about position or time.
They are usually placed **before** nouns and pronouns.
Most prepositions are quite small words.

A ***The passage below is part of the story about Jack and the Beanstalk. Read the passage and underline ten different prepositions in it.***

The giant sat down and asked his wife to bring him his hen. She went out and soon came back, carrying a beautiful hen in her arms. She put it on the table in front of the giant. "Lay!" roared the giant and the hen laid an egg.

Jack was peeping from the cupboard. He saw that the egg was made of pure gold. He told himself that if he could have the hen, he and his mother would never be poor again.

Then the giant and his wife ate their dinner. They had so much to eat and drink that they soon fell asleep. Jack quickly took the hen from the table and ran out to the beanstalk as fast as he could. He climbed down the beanstalk with the hen under one arm.

When he reached the bottom, he rushed into his mother's cottage and put the hen on the table. "Lay!" he said. His mother was surprised to see the hen lay a beautiful golden egg.

Jack and his mother became rich and lived happily for many years.

© 2012 Scholastic Education International (S) Pte Ltd ISBN 978-81-8477-746-8

B Fill in the blanks with suitable prepositions. The pictures will help you.

Prepositions that tell you about time

on at past since for by

1. The time is half ______________ two.

2. I have been waiting ______________ one o'clock.

3. Let's meet ______________ three o'clock.

4. He will be here ______________ five o'clock.

5. It is my birthday ______________ Friday.

6. I had to wait ______________ three hours.

Prepositions that tell you about position

on	under	into
behind	over	near

7. The lizard was ______________ the rock.

8. The lizard was ______________ the rock.

9. The lizard was ______________ the rock.

10. The lizard ran ______________ the rock.

11. The lizard fell ______________ the mud.

12. The lizard dug ______________ the rock.

© 2012 Scholastic Education International (S) Pte Ltd ISBN 978-81-8477-746-8

C *Look at the pictures and answer the questions.*

1. Where is Mrs Lee?

____

____

2. Where is the squirrel?

____

____

3. Where is Sue standing?

____

____

4. Where is the picture?

____

____

5. Where are the children playing?

____

____

6. Where are the balloons?

____

____

© 2012 Scholastic Education International (S) Pte Ltd ISBN 978-81-8477-746-8

D *Fill in the blanks with prepositions of place or time. You have to use some of the prepositions more than once.*

Time

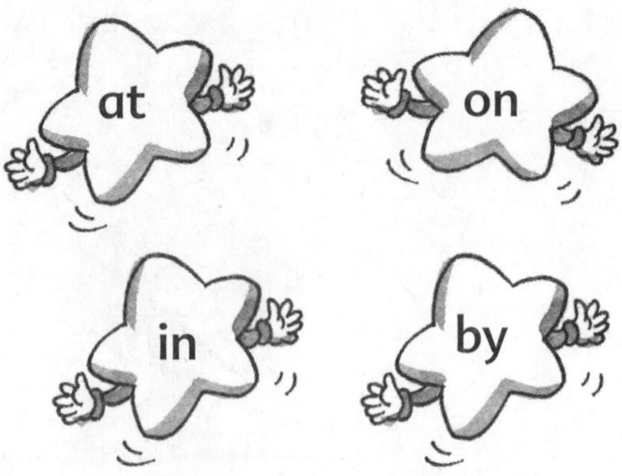

Place

1. The concert started ________ 8:00 p.m.
2. Grandpa and Grandma were married ________ 1939.
3. Our exams begin ________ Monday.
4. The boys like playing ________ the stream.
5. He saw a lot of animals ________ the zoo.
6. We went rowing ________ the lake.
7. The monkey is riding ________ the back of the tiger.
8. He met his friend ________ the bus stop.
9. The team is leaving ________ Singapore next week.
10. The bird flew ________ the roof of the house.
11. The children will be home ________ noon.
12. The painter worked quickly and completed his job ________ a few days.

© 2012 Scholastic Education International (S) Pte Ltd ISBN 978-81-8477-746-8

14 am, is, are

Grammar Help

You use **am** with **I**.

You use **is** with **he**, **she** and **it**, or with **singular nouns**.

You use **are** with **you**, **we** and **they**, or with **plural nouns**.

A ***Read about Jack and his family. Then fill in each blank with am, is or are.***

My name (1) __________ Jack and I (2) __________ six years old.

This (3) __________ my father. He (4) __________ a manager in a supermarket. This (5) __________ my mother. She (6) __________ a teacher in a primary school. These (7) __________ my brother, Daniel, and sisters, Sue and Catherine. Daniel (8) __________ eight, Sue is seven, and Catherine is nine. We all attend the same school.

We have a dog called Ludo. It (9) __________ a German Shepherd.

This (10) __________ my dad's new car. He drives us to school every morning.

© 2012 Scholastic Education International (S) Pte Ltd ISBN 978-81-8477-746-8

B Fill in each blank with **am**, **is** or **are**.

1. I __________ a student at Winton Primary School.
2. She __________ a beautiful girl.
3. It __________ a hot day today.
4. They __________ late again.
5. You __________ taller than I am.
6. He __________ a librarian.
7. She __________ a taxi-driver.
8. We __________ from the Police Force.

9. It __________ already dark.
10. Little Red Riding Hood __________ at her grandmother's cottage.
11. She sees someone in her grandmother's bed and asks, "Who __________ you?"
12. The wolf replies, "I __________ your granny."

© 2012 Scholastic Education International (S) Pte Ltd ISBN 978-81-8477-746-8

C *Fill in each blank with* ***is not*** *or* ***are not.***

1. My uncle is a doctor.

   He ____is not____ an engineer.

2. These are eagles.

   They __________ parrots.

3. The boy is six years old.

   He __________ seven years old.

4. They are soldiers.

   They __________ police officers.

5. This is a crocodile.

   It __________ a snake.

6. The weather is hot.

   It __________ cold.

7. The earth is round.

   It __________ square.

8. These dogs are sleeping.

   They __________ barking.

© 2012 Scholastic Education International (S) Pte Ltd ISBN 978-81-8477-746-8

D ***Write the short form of each set of words on the left in the space on the right. Remember to use an apostrophe to show where the missing letter should be.***

1. I am — I'm not
2. you are — not
3. he is — not
4. she is — not
5. it is — not
6. we are — not
7. they are — not
8. is not — he
9. are not — you

© 2012 Scholastic Education International (S) Pte Ltd ISBN 978-81-8477-746-8

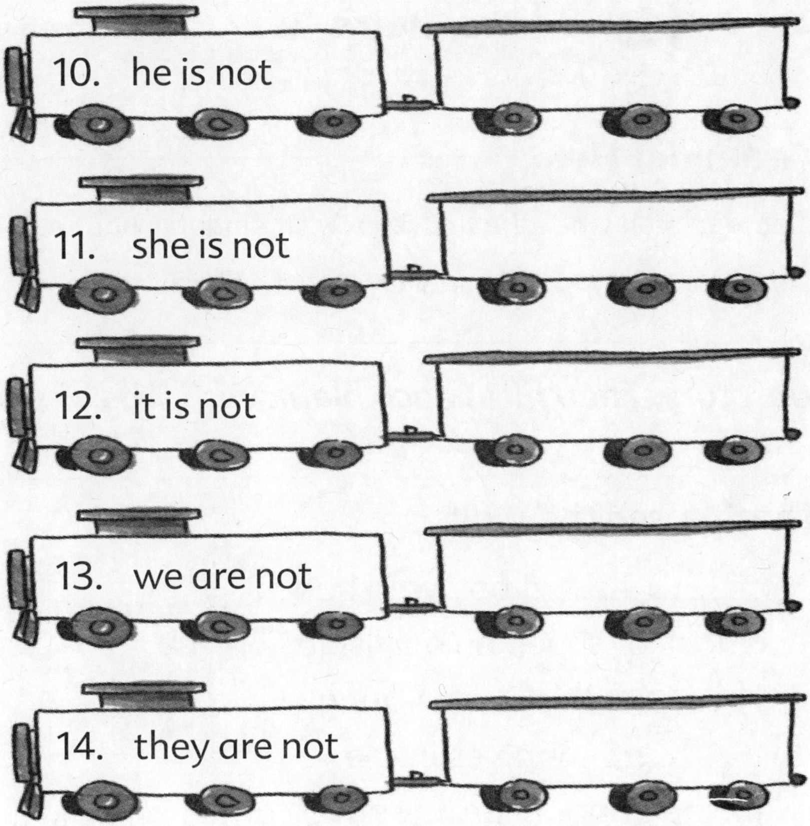

Complete each sentence using the short form of the words in brackets.

15. ____________________ (She is) my cousin.

16. This pencil ____________________ (is not) sharp.

17. ____________________ (I am) the tallest in class.

18. ____________________ (They are) not butterflies.

19. My dad ____________________ (is not) at home.

20. Sam and Peter ____________________ (are not) in the library.

© 2012 Scholastic Education International (S) Pte Ltd ISBN 978-81-8477-746-8

15 was, were

Grammar Help

You use **was** with **I**, **he**, **she** and **it**, or with **singular nouns**.

You use **were** with **you**, **we** and **they**, or with **plural nouns**.

A ***Read the story. Then fill in each blank with* was *or* were*.***

The Boy and the Wolf

Once there (1) __________ a boy who had to look after a flock of sheep on a hillside. The shepherd boy (2) __________ young and there (3) __________ wolves in the area. So his kind neighbours promised to come to his aid if he saw a wolf. All he had to do (4) __________ to shout "Wolf!" loudly and they would come to help him.

One day, the boy shouted "Wolf!" just for fun. All his neighbours came rushing to help him. They (5) __________ very angry with him when they realized there (6) __________ no wolf.

The next morning, the boy again shouted "Wolf!" even though there (7) __________ no wolf. Again the neighbours came. They (8) __________ even angrier when they realized they had been tricked a second time.

Not long after this, a wolf really came. It began to attack the sheep. The boy shouted "Wolf! Wolf!" at the top of his voice many times, but nobody came to his aid. The neighbours thought he (9) __________ trying to trick them again.

© 2012 Scholastic Education International (S) Pte Ltd ISBN 978-81-8477-746-8

B *Fill in each blank with **was or were.***

1. It __________ a very cold day yesterday.
2. I __________ top of the class last year.
3. I went to Mark's house but he __________ not in.
4. She __________ absent from school yesterday.
5. He __________ in the library an hour ago.
6. We __________ neighbours before I moved to Jurong.
7. They __________ here just now.
8. She __________ very unhappy when you broke her guitar.
9. Jack and his mother __________ very poor.
10. Joe and Sue __________ in the same class last year.

C *Complete this paragraph by filling in each blank with **was or were.***

Where (1) __________ you yesterday? I needed help with my maths. I looked for Bob in the library. He (2) __________ not there. I looked for Kim in the playground. She (3) __________ not there. I looked for Sook Leng and Zahara in the classroom. They (4) __________ not there. So I went home. Mum and Dad (5) __________ able to help me.

© 2012 Scholastic Education International (S) Pte Ltd ISBN 978-81-8477-746-8

D ***Write the short form of each set of words on the left in the space on the right. The pronoun is given.***

1.	I was not	I
2.	she was not	she
3.	he was not	he
4.	it was not	it
5.	you were not	you
6.	we were not	we
7.	they were not	they

Write the short form of the words in brackets in each sentence.

8. It ____________ (was not) cold yesterday.
9. Jill and Sue ____________ (were not) in the same class last year.
10. He ____________ (was not) at the bus stop this morning.
11. We ____________ (were not) at the party.
12. Pinocchio ____________ (was not) a bad boy.
13. I ____________ (was not) angry with him.
14. They ____________ (were not) unkind to us.
15. You ____________ (were not) very happy to see Tom just now.

© 2012 Scholastic Education International (S) Pte Ltd ISBN 978-81-8477-746-8

16 can, may, should

A ***Choose the most suitable word to complete each sentence. Do not use any word more than once.***

carry	walk	answer	keep	sing
speak	climb	play	watch	go

1. Look, he can ______________ on his hands!
2. The children can all ______________ very well. They are in the school choir.
3. Peter can ______________ all the questions. They are too easy for him.
4. My grandparents can ______________ English very well.
5. Cats can ______________ trees. My pet cat climbed that tree yesterday.
6. Sue and Kathy can ______________ the piano. They have had piano lessons for two years.
7. Can I ______________ television after dinner? I have no homework to do tonight.
8. Can we ______________ home now? We have completed our work.
9. Can you ______________ this box of books? It is too heavy for me.
10. Can you ______________ a secret? I need to tell someone my problem.

© 2012 Scholastic Education International (S) Pte Ltd ISBN 978-81-8477-746-8

Grammar Help

The short form of **cannot** is **can't**.

B ***Fill in each blank with can or can't.***

1. I can swim, but Joe ____________ .
2. "____________ I talk to you later? I have to finish this exercise before ten."
   "Yes, you ____________ . I'll call you again after ten."
3. "____________ you read the words on the poster from here?"
   "No, I ____________ . I am not wearing my glasses."
4. Dogs ____________ climb trees, but cats ____________ .
5. I am full. I ____________ finish the food.
6. ____________ you help me? I don't know the way to the station.
7. How many languages ____________ you speak? I know you speak at least two languages.
8. Run as fast as you ____________ . Try to win the race for our class.
9. Not all birds ____________ fly. Ostriches ____________ .
10. It is raining, so we ____________ go to the playground.

© 2012 Scholastic Education International (S) Pte Ltd ISBN 978-81-8477-746-8

C *Fill in each blank with **may** or **may not.***

1. "__________ I come in? I need to talk to you now."
   "Yes, do come in and take a seat."

2. You __________ leave now if you wish. I won't keep you back.

3. There's thunder and lightning. It __________ rain soon.

4. It's already so late. Jane __________ come.

5. I like the computer game very much. But Dad __________ allow me to buy it.

6. Children, you __________ all sit down. Then we will start the lesson.

7. John __________ come to the party, but Peter __________.

8. We __________ have enough coins for the bus fare. Let's ask the shopkeeper to change this five-dollar note.

9. Put down the knife. You __________ hurt yourself.

10. "__________ I leave the room to go to the canteen?"

    "No, you __________! You must finish the exercise first."

11. Speak softly. You __________ wake the baby.

12. You __________ be allowed in if you are late for the concert.

© 2012 Scholastic Education International (S) Pte Ltd ISBN 978-81-8477-746-8

Grammar Help

The short form of **should not** is **shouldn't**.

D ***Fill in each blank with should or shouldn't, whichever is more suitable.***

1. "Do you think I ______________ lend him the money?"

   "No, you ______________. He will spend it on useless things."

2. We ______________ use the lift if there's a fire. The lift may get stuck and trap us.

3. We ______________ tell Mum where we are going. She will worry if she does not know where we are.

4. Children ______________ eat too many sweets. They will spoil their appetite.

5. We ______________ look both ways before crossing the road.

6. Students ______________ be attentive in class. Then they will learn more.

7. We ______________ be kind to small animals. They cannot defend themselves.

8. People ______________ tell lies. They may harm others with their lies.

9. It's getting late. We ______________ leave now.

10. You ______________ overfeed the goldfish. They will die of overeating.

© 2012 Scholastic Education International (S) Pte Ltd ISBN 978-81-8477-746-8

17 The Present Tense

Grammar Help

A **verb** in the **present tense** tells you that an action is happening now or it is done as a habit.

A ***Complete each sentence with the most suitable verb from the box. Do not use any verb more than once.***

live	close	fit	make	washes	goes
reads	cross	like	make	takes	borrows	helps

1. Uncle Jerry ______________ his car once a week.
2. The children ______________ ice cream.
3. John sometimes ______________ my bicycle.
4. These shoes ______________ me well.
5. All shops in this area ______________ on Sundays.
6. Tom, you ______________ too much noise.
7. Dad ______________ us to the pool every Sunday.
8. We never ______________ the road without looking at both sides of the road for traffic.
9. My brother sometimes ______________ me with my homework.
10. We ______________ near the fire station.
11. Mum ______________ the newspaper in the evening.
12. Mr Parker ______________ to work by bus.

© 2012 Scholastic Education International (S) Pte Ltd ISBN 978-81-8477-746-8

Grammar Help

You also use the **present tense** to talk about things that are always true.

B ***Read the passage and underline the verbs in the present tense.***

The Giant Panda

The giant panda is a very rare animal. It lives in the bamboo forests on some mountain slopes in China.

It is as big as a bear and has a white chubby body with black legs. It has a black patch around each eye.

The giant panda feeds only on bamboo shoots, stems and leaves. But the areas where bamboo grows well have become smaller. So the Chinese grow bamboo in special areas for the giant panda to eat.

© 2012 Scholastic Education International (S) Pte Ltd ISBN 978-81-8477-746-8

C ***Complete each sentence with the most suitable verb from the box. Do not use any verb more than once.***

are	grow	taste	runs	live	is
hear	make	build	eat	lay	cry

1. The Earth ________________ round.
2. Many birds ________________ their nests in trees.
3. Frogs ________________ their eggs in water.
4. Snakes ________________ reptiles.
5. We ________________ with our ears.
6. Fish ________________ in water.
7. A tiger ________________ faster than an elephant.
8. Babies ________________ when they are hungry.
9. Lizards ________________ small insects.
10. Plants ________________ from seeds.
11. Two and ten ________________ twelve.
12. Lemons ________________ sour.

© 2012 Scholastic Education International (S) Pte Ltd ISBN 978-81-8477-746-8

D ***Answer these questions.***
Use verbs in the present tense.

1. What is your name?

 ____

2. Where do you live?

 ____

 ____

3. How do you go to school?

 ____

4. What do you do after school?

 ____

 ____

5. What games do you play?

 ____

 ____

6. How do you feel right now?

 ____

 ____

© 2012 Scholastic Education International (S) Pte Ltd ISBN 978-81-8477-746-8

18 The Past Tense

Grammar Help

Verbs in the **past tense** tell you about actions that happened in the past. Many such verbs end in ***-ed***.

A ***Read this story and underline the verbs in the past tense.***

The Wolf in a Sheepskin

There was once a wolf who wanted to kill a sheep for dinner. He found a sheepskin and wrapped it round himself. Then he crept into a field full of sheep and pretended to graze all day just as they did.

When night came, the shepherd rounded the sheep into a pen. He did not know that one of them was really a wolf. The wolf walked round the pen, looking for the fattest sheep to kill.

Unfortunately for him, however, the shepherd came back to the pen to look for a sheep for his dinner. He picked a large one. To his surprise, it was a wolf wearing a sheepskin!

© 2012 Scholastic Education International (S) Pte Ltd ISBN 978-81-8477-746-8

B ***Complete each sentence with the most suitable verb from the box. Do not use any verb more than once.***

hit	built	began	baked	changed
lost	visited	died	saw	celebrated

1. Mum ____________________ a butter cake.

2. A ball ____________________ John on the head.

3. Dinosaurs ____________________ out millions of years ago.

4. We ____________________ the film last week.

5. They ____________________ Paris a year ago.

6. Norlin ____________________ her birthday yesterday.

7. The deaf man ____________________ his hearing when he was a boy.

8. This is the house that Jack ____________________ .

9. I ____________________ piano lessons last year.

10. The frog ____________________ into a handsome prince.

© 2012 Scholastic Education International (S) Pte Ltd ISBN 978-81-8477-746-8

C *Look at each picture. Complete each sentence with a suitable verb in the past tense.*

1. Last night I ______________ my favourite TV show.

2. David ______________ his dog a bone.

3. I ______________ a long letter to my friend in Japan.

4. Our team ______________ yesterday's football match.

5. Jane ______________ some books from the library.

6. Jack ______________ up the beanstalk to the giant's castle.

7. We ______________ the dishes after dinner.

8. The little girl ______________ at the funny clown.

© 2012 Scholastic Education International (S) Pte Ltd ISBN 978-81-8477-746-8

19 The Future Tense

Grammar Help

Verbs in the **future tense** tell you about actions that will happen after the present. A verb in the **future tense** is formed by putting **shall** or **will** in front of the infinitive (base form of the verb).

Example: **shall**/**will** come

A ***Read Peter's diary and underline all the verbs in the future tense.***

Miss Lee told us this morning that our school will stage a play called "Hansel and Gretel" during the school holidays. Miss Lee will direct the play. We shall take part in the play.

Mark will play the role of the woodcutter. Susan will take the part of the stepmother. I shall act Hansel. Kate will be Gretel.

The school will invite all our parents to the play. The play will be fun and everyone will enjoy it.

© 2012 Scholastic Education International (S) Pte Ltd ISBN 978-81-8477-746-8

Grammar Help

You use **shall** or **will** with **I** and **we**.
You use **will** with **he, she, it, you** and **they**.

B ***Complete the sentences with verbs in the future tense. Use the verbs in the box only once each.***

play	**use**	**help**	**hurt**	**take**
visit	**go**	**have**	**be**	**grow**
start	**leave**	**watch**	**paint**	**get**

1. I am seven years old. Next year I ________________ eight.
2. Our exams ________________ next week.
3. I ________________ my bath later.
4. We ________________ to the beach tomorrow.
5. You ________________ fat if you continue to eat so much.
6. We ________________ for the airport after dinner tonight.
7. Give me the knife. You ________________ yourself.
8. ________ we ____________ James in the hospital tomorrow?
9. ________ we ____________ a game of chess after school?
10. ________ you ____________ me with this sum?
11. More people ________________ the Internet in the future.
12. They ________________ the house this weekend.
13. You ________________ time for breakfast if you get up earlier tomorrow.
14. We must hurry. It ________________ dark soon.
15. Jim ________________ television after finishing his homework.

© 2012 Scholastic Education International (S) Pte Ltd ISBN 978-81-8477-746-8

Grammar Help

You use **will** with the infinitive (base form of the verb) to talk about things you plan to do.

C ***Look at each picture and write what the child is planning to do on the weekend. The first sentence is completed as an example.***

1. Sue will visit her grandmother.

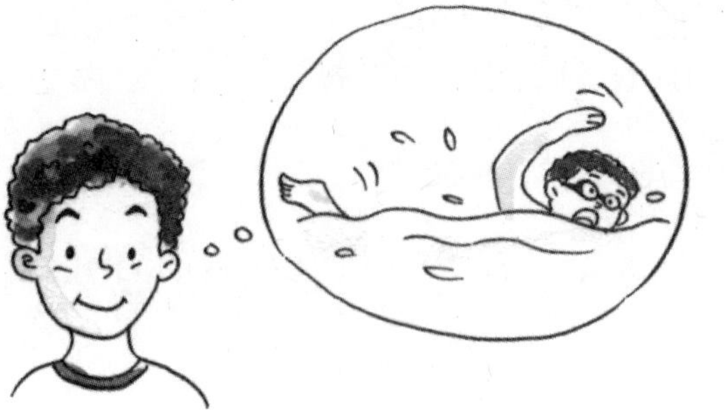

2. Omar ____________________

____

3. Li Ping ____________________

____

4. Mark ____________________

____

5. Kim ____________________

____

6. Nathan ____________________

____

© 2012 Scholastic Education International (S) Pte Ltd ISBN 978-81-8477-746-8

20 Adverbs

Grammar Help

Adverbs tell you more about verbs. Some adverbs tell you **how** things happen.

A ***Complete each sentence with the most suitable adverb from the box. Use each adverb only once.***

safely	**carefully**	**fairly**	**sweetly**	**easily**
neatly	**happily**	**softly**	**quickly**	**quietly**

1. There is a bird singing ________________ outside the window.
2. Please arrange the books ________________ on the top shelf.
3. We walked ________________ into the dark room so as not to wake the children.
4. The plane landed ________________ at the airport.
5. Dad always drives ________________; so we feel safe with him.
6. The children shared the biscuits ________________ among themselves.
7. When the clock struck twelve, Cinderella ________________ ran out of the palace.
8. The prince and princess got married and lived ________________ ever after.
9. The leopard caught the sick antelope ________________.
10. Sandra spoke so ________________ Miss Lee could not hear her.

© 2012 Scholastic Education International (S) Pte Ltd ISBN 978-81-8477-746-8

Grammar Help

Some adverbs tell you **where** things happen.

B ***Complete each sentence with the most suitable adverb from the box. Do not use any adverb more than once.***

outside	everywhere	over	here
away	downstairs	close	there

1. The rain has stopped. Let's go ______________ and play.
2. Kathy's house is not far from ______________ ; we will reach it in five minutes.
3. Have you seen my book? I put it on that table a little while ago but it is not ______________ now.
4. We go ______________ by car because it's a long walk to the nearest bus stop.
5. Sorry, the doctor is ______________ ; he won't be back till Friday.
6. Don't cross the road. He's coming ______________ .
7. Mum and Dad are watching television ______________ ; they will come up only after the show.
8. Don't stand too ______________ to the fire! It will scorch your clothes.

© 2012 Scholastic Education International (S) Pte Ltd ISBN 978-81-8477-746-8

Grammar Help

Some adverbs tell you **when** things happen.

C ***Complete each sentence with the most suitable adverb from the box. Do not use any adverb more than once.***

soon	tomorrow	before	now	late
today	yesterday	early	yet	first

1. I have seen that man ______________ . He came to our school last week.
2. John, get up ______________ . It's eight o'clock.
3. The concert is going to start ______________ . Let's take our seats.
4. Sue celebrated her birthday ______________ .
5. The boys will be back ______________ after a week at the camp.
6. Tom arrived ______________ because he missed the bus.
7. Grandma always gets up ______________ to prepare breakfast for us.
8. ______________ we are going to the beach instead of the zoo.
9. The doctor will see the boy with the broken arm ______________ ; the other patients are willing to wait.
10. Don't serve dinner ______________ ; the children aren't ready to eat.

© 2012 Scholastic Education International (S) Pte Ltd ISBN 978-81-8477-746-8

D ***Read the story and underline eight adverbs that describe how things were done.***

Cinderella and the Prince

It was almost midnight, but Cinderella did not notice this. She and the prince were talking cheerfully to each other. Then the clock began to strike. Cinderella quickly stood up and ran out of the ballroom.

As she was running down the steps, Cinderella carelessly dropped one of her glass slippers. But she ran on, anxiously hoping to reach her carriage in time.

When she went near, however, her carriage and horses all disappeared. Hopelessly, Cinderella continued her run home. As she ran, her ball gown changed back into her old ragged dress.

At last she was safely back in her kitchen. She sat down slowly, and thought sadly how her night out had come to an end.

© 2012 Scholastic Education International (S) Pte Ltd ISBN 978-81-8477-746-8

21 Conjunctions

Grammar Help

Three words you can use to join words and sentences are **and**, **or** and **but**. These words are called **conjunctions**.

A ***Read this short play and underline the conjunctions.***

Amy & May:	Mum, can we go outside and play?
Mum:	Well, the day is fine but it is windy and cold. Don't go outside or you might catch cold.
May:	Please, Mum. We're bored and I've finished my homework.
Mum:	Then you could help Dad or Grandma, or you could clean your room.
Amy:	We've already offered to help but they said no, and we've cleaned our room.
Mum:	Then be sure you get back before three o'clock.
Amy & May:	Thanks, Mum!

© 2012 Scholastic Education International (S) Pte Ltd ISBN 978-81-8477-746-8

Grammar Help

Another name for **conjunctions** is **connectors**.

B *Join each pair of sentences using **or, but** or **and**.*

1. Is that an eagle?
   Is that a hawk?

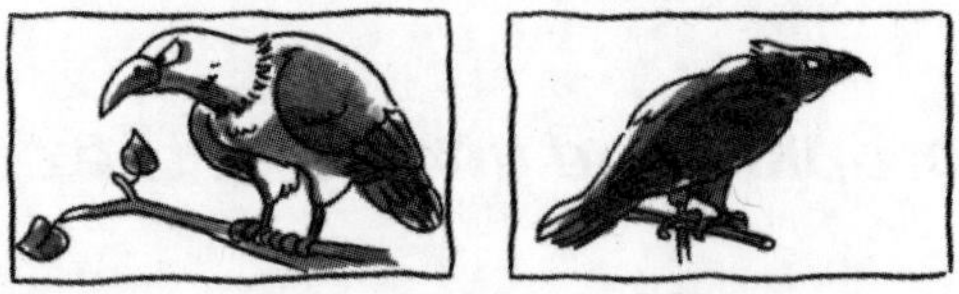

   Is that an eagle ________ a hawk?

2. Summer is usually hot.
   Winter is usually cold.

   Summer is usually hot ________ winter is usually cold.

3. Would you like tea?
   Would you like coffee?

   Would you like tea ________ coffee?

4. This is a story about a wolf.
   This is also a story about three pigs.

   This is a story about a wolf ________ three pigs.

5. I play the piano.
   My brother plays the drums.

   I play the piano ________ my brother plays the drums.

© 2012 Scholastic Education International (S) Pte Ltd ISBN 978-81-8477-746-8

C ***Make a sentence with the words in each pair of balloons and using the conjunction* but*. The first one is done as an example.***

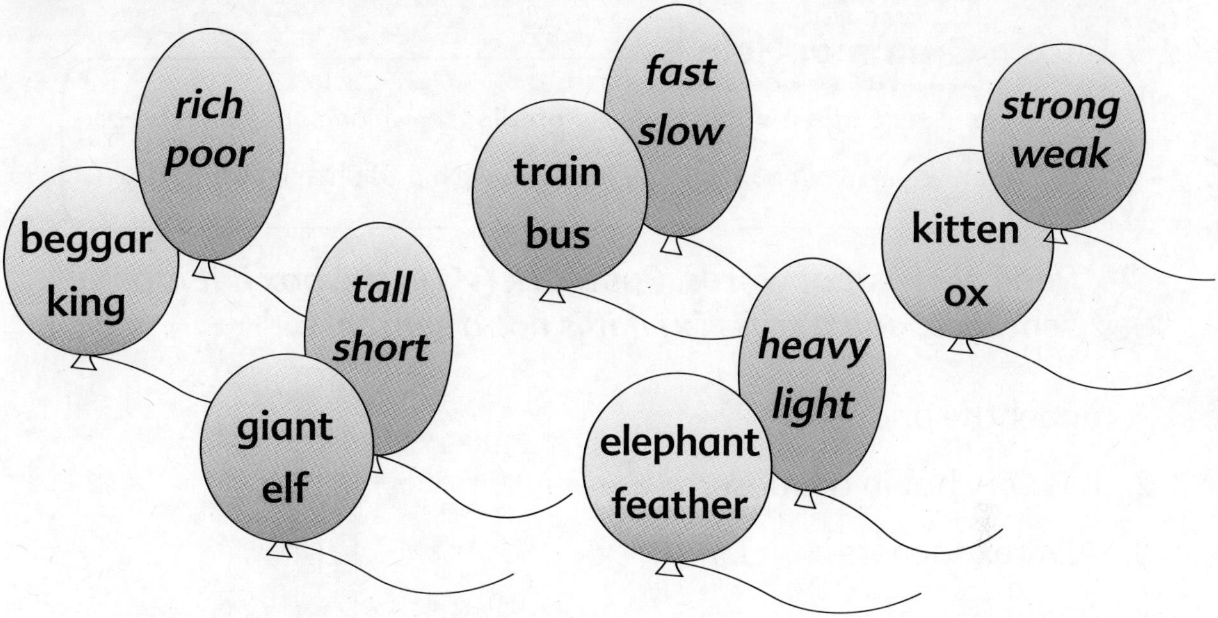

1. A king is rich but a beggar is poor.

2. ______________________________

3. ______________________________

4. ______________________________

5. ______________________________

© 2012 Scholastic Education International (S) Pte Ltd ISBN 978-81-8477-746-8

22 Sentences

Grammar Help

A sentence has a **subject** and a **predicate**, which contains a **verb**.
When you write a sentence, you start with a capital letter.

A ***Read each set of words. Put a tick (✓) in the box if it is a sentence, and a cross (x) if it is not a sentence.***

1. under the bridge ☐
2. It is very hot in the desert. ☐
3. All the teachers ☐
4. Please sit down. ☐
5. Mum is in the kitchen. ☐
6. Whose bag is this? ☐
7. next week ☐
8. just a minute ☐
9. Get up! ☐
10. Dave's father ☐

B ***Underline the subject in each sentence and circle the verb in the predicate.***

1. Uncle Charles bought a poodle.
2. Dave won the first prize for Mathematics.
3. Miss Lee teaches English in a primary school.
4. Dad is enjoying his coffee.

© 2012 Scholastic Education International (S) Pte Ltd ISBN 978-81-8477-746-8

5. The children are building a sandcastle.
6. They are eating their dinner.
7. Sue is reading a storybook.
8. I hurt my leg yesterday.
9. Hens lay eggs.
10. Tom is flying his kite.

C ***Make three sentences with each group of subject and predicate. The first group is done as an example.***

1.

Subject	Predicate
Children	are afraid of thunder and lightning.
	like ice cream.
	must not talk to strangers.

(a) Children are afraid of thunder and lightning.

(b) Children like ice cream.

(c) Children must not talk to strangers.

2.

Subject	Predicate
An elephant	has a long nose.
	is a big and strong animal.
	can help people do work.

(a) ______________________

(b) ______________________

(c) ______________________

© 2012 Scholastic Education International (S) Pte Ltd ISBN 978-81-8477-746-8

3.

Mum
Our teacher
Uncle John

→ asked us to keep quiet.

(a) ____________________

(b) ____________________

(c) ____________________

4.

They
Mr and Mrs Ross
The schoolchildren

→ are waiting for the bus.

(a) ____________________

(b) ____________________

(c) ____________________

5.

John and his dog →

are in the garden.
like to play in the rain.
go to the park every day.

(a) ____________________

(b) ____________________

(c) ____________________

© 2012 Scholastic Education International (S) Pte Ltd ISBN 978-81-8477-746-8

D ***Match each subject in the left column with the most suitable predicate in the right column to make a sentence. Write the sentences on the lines below.***

Subject	Predicate
1. Some birds	are swimming in the pool.
2. The dog	are chasing the thief.
3. I	often fight.
4. Uncle Tom	cannot fly.
5. This book	is barking at the stranger.
6. The police officers	was very windy yesterday.
7. Dogs and cats	am listening to music.
8. The children	bought Peter a present.
9. These books	is very interesting.
10. The weather	have lots of pictures.

1. ______________________________

2. ______________________________

3. ______________________________

4. ______________________________

5. ______________________________

6. ______________________________

7. ______________________________

8. ______________________________

9. ______________________________

10. ______________________________

© 2012 Scholastic Education International (S) Pte Ltd ISBN 978-81-8477-746-8

Revision Test

Section 1 (40 marks)

A ***Fill in each blank with a suitable word from the box. You may need to use two of the words more than once each.*** **(5 marks)**

a	an	the

1. There is ____________ apple in the basket.
2. Please read me ____________ story about the lion and the mouse.
3. Tom is my friend but I don't like ____________ boy with him.
4. Do you have ____________ pencil I could borrow, please?
5. The cave was guarded by ____________ ugly giant.

B ***Fill in each blank with a suitable word from the box.*** **(5 marks)**

am	is	are	was	were

6. My mother ____________ happy to help in the school library.
7. Tom and Sam ____________ the very best of friends.
8. I ____________ not allowed to come to your party tomorrow.
9. My friends ____________ not at the library when I arrived.
10. My grandfather ____________ a train driver a long time ago.

© 2012 Scholastic Education International (S) Pte Ltd ISBN 978-81-8477-746-8

C *Fill in each blank with a suitable word from the box. Use each word only once.* (5 marks)

dirty	strong	happy	lazy	noisy

11. The ____________ man lifted the log and threw it out of his way.
12. The mother smiled at her ____________ baby laughing in his cot.
13. You must wash your ____________ hands before eating.
14. The teacher told her ____________ class to be quiet.
15. In our class the ____________ students seldom finish their work.

D *Look at the picture and fill in each blank with a suitable word from the box. Use each word only once.* (5 marks)

between	in	on	under	near

16. The birds are chirping ____________ their cage.
17. The cat is sleeping ____________ the pillows on John's bed.
18. John's shoes are ____________ his chair.
19. A beach ball is ____________ the lamp.
20. John's dog is playing with a ball ____________ the mat.

© 2012 Scholastic Education International (S) Pte Ltd ISBN 978-81-8477-746-8

E *Circle the correct word in the brackets for each sentence.* (10 marks)

21. Hello, Sam. I am six years old. How old are (we, you, they)?
22. Sam and I are good friends. (We, Us, You) have been friends for one year.
23. I ate three (cherries, cherry, cherrys) for dessert at dinner.
24. Before going to bed, (she, he, I) brushes his teeth.
25. The bull and cow had twin (ewes, lambs, calves).
26. "Is there a bus to my house?" "No, there (is, aren't, isn't)."
27. My friends and I play together. (They, Us, We) like to go to the park.
28. This is my cap; so (that, these, those) one must be yours.
29. When I found (his, her, their) wallet, I returned it to him.
30. Dinosaurs (live, lived, lives) a long time ago.

F *Fill in each blank with the correct word and write its number in the brackets.* (10 marks)

31. I had to climb ______________ to reach the attic.

    (1) upstairs (2) downstairs
    (3) inside (4) outside ( )

32. The ewes and their ______________ are grazing in the field.

    (1) flock (2) sheep
    (3) lambs (4) calves ( )

33. "Are there any biscuits in the jar?" "No, there ______________."

    (1) is (2) are
    (3) aren't (4) isn't ( )

© 2012 Scholastic Education International (S) Pte Ltd ISBN 978-81-8477-746-8

34. My friends and I all ______________ in the same housing estate now.

(1) live (2) lived
(3) living (4) lives ( )

35. I don't think you ______________ climb that tree; it's too tall.

(1) shall (2) should
(3) couldn't (4) shouldn't ( )

36. Mum goes to that shop because it ______________ delicious sausages.

(1) selling (2) sold
(3) sell (4) sells ( )

37. He picked up the baby bird ______________ and gently put it back in the nest.

(1) carelessly (2) carefully
(3) helplessly (4) helpfully ( )

38. I received your letter ______________ .

(1) next week (2) tonight
(3) yesterday (4) tomorrow ( )

39. You could stay here with me ______________ go there with Sue.

(1) so (2) but
(3) and (4) or ( )

40. Winter here is unpleasant because it's very cold ______________ summer is pleasant because it's warm.

(1) so (2) or
(3) and (4) but ( )

© 2012 Scholastic Education International (S) Pte Ltd ISBN 978-81-8477-746-8

Section 2 (10 marks)

G ***Fill in each blank in the passage with the most suitable word from the box. There will be five words left over when you finish.*** **(10 marks)**

he	weeds	an	doesn't	are
his	shelves	on	outside	of
is	the	in	shelf	a

It is ten o'clock (41) ____________ Sunday morning.

Mrs Lang and her children (42) ____________ cleaning the house. Mrs Lang wears (43) ____________ apron when she cleans the house. Kim is washing the dishes, but Tom (44) ____________ want to dry them because (45) ____________ prefers to mop the floor. Sue is dusting all the (46) ____________ in the library. She will put the books back when she has finished.

Mr Lang is (47) ____________ the garden weeding. He is pulling up (48) ____________ and putting them in a bucket.

Spot, (49) ____________ family dog, is fast asleep in the shade (50) ____________ a tree.

Section 1:	/40
Section 2:	/10
TOTAL	/50

© 2012 Scholastic Education International (S) Pte Ltd ISBN 978-81-8477-746-8

Page 6

A 1. carnations 2. daisies
3. lilies 4. orchids
5. roses 6. sunflowers
7. tulips

Page 7

B 1. a, e, i, o, u
No. of vowels: 5
2. All letters except the vowels
No. of consonants: 21

C 1. a a e 2. u e a 3. o i
4. o i o 5. o o a 6. u i

Page 8

D 2. fan, (fen), fin, fun
3. pan, pen, pin, pun
4. (dag), dig, dog, dug
5. net, nit, not, nut
6. map, mop
7. lag, leg, log, lug
8. cat, cot, cut

E *Answers may vary—Teacher to check.*

Page 9

A

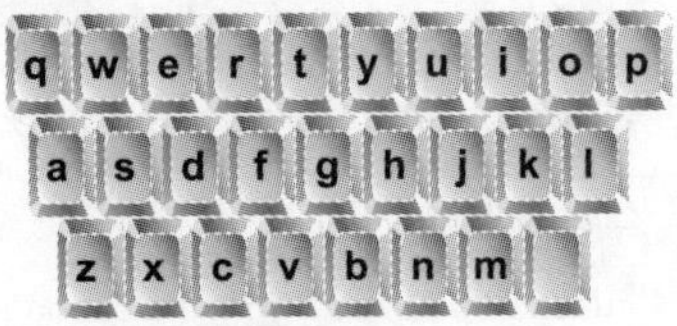

B *Teacher to check.*

Page 10

C 1. *Teacher to check.*
2. **b**ird **k**ite **n**est **d**ragonfly **f**lower **t**ree **g**love **c**loud

Page 11

3. *Suggested answers:*
Andrew **S**andra **T**heresa
Henry **K**evin **M**iriam
4. *See below:*

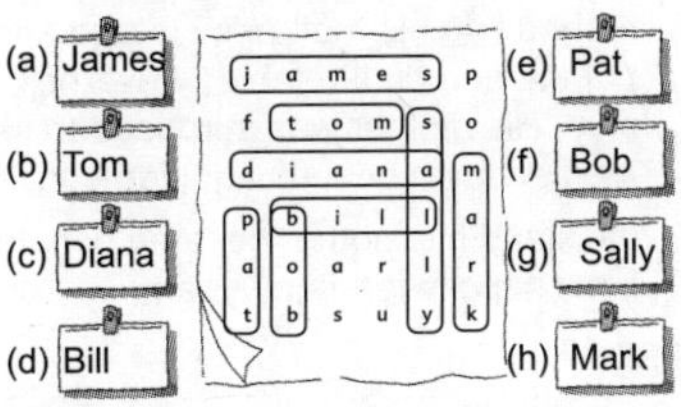

Page 12

D *Teacher to check.*

E Mark Chen
25 Madison Avenue
New York 10016
United States of America

Page 13

A Once there was an old man and an old woman. They lived in a little house on the top of a hill. They felt lonely.

One day, the old woman had an idea. She would make a boy to keep them company. So she mixed an egg and some ginger powder with a large bowl of flour. She made the shape of a little boy with the dough. Then she put the 'boy' in the oven to bake.

After an hour, the old woman opened the oven door to take the boy out. To her surprise, the Gingerbread Boy jumped up and ran out of the house and down the hill. Very sadly, the old woman watched him run away.

Page 14

B an eagle a parrot an owl
a trainer a feather a camera
a mouse a pelican a swan

Page 15

C 1. an, a 2. an, a 3. a, an
4. a, an 5. a, an 6. an, a

Page 16

D **The Three Billy Goats Gruff**
the, the The the, a
the, an the, the
The Selfish Giant
a the, a The, the, a
Jack and the Beanstalk
the, the an the, the
a, the, an

Page 17

A 1. road/street 2. door
3. story/book 4. police officer
5. monkey 6. television
7. driver 8. violin

Page 18

B *Answers may vary.*
1. fish, frog, footprint, fountain, flower, fence
2. swan, swing, slide, skateboard, seesaw
3. boy, butterfly, book, bench, bicycle

Page 19

4. *Answers may vary.*
5. *Answers may vary—including* path, lamp, bush, litter bin, grass
6. man, woman, boy, girl, people, parents, children

Page 20

C **Across**
1. dog 3. aeroplane 4. car
5. pen 6. orange 8. key
Down
1. door 2. cake
3. arrow 5. pear
7. nose

Page 21

A 1. First Bank, United Bank
2. First Bank Building, Star Cinema, Lido Cinema, United Bank/City Library Building
3. Prince Road, Hill Street, Beach Road
4. capital

Page 22

B *In the calendar, students to write:* Monday, Tuesday, Wednesday, Thursday, Friday, Saturday
1. Sunday 2. Thursday
3. proper 4. capital

Page 23

C *In the spaces, students to write:* February, March, April, May, June, July, August, September, October, November, December

Page 24

D *In the chart, students to write:*
People: Alice, Pinocchio, James, Dr Lee
Places: Winton Primary School, King's Road, York Hospital, National Zoo
Books and Movies: *The Golden Goose, The Lion King*
Special Days: Saturday, Mother's Day, Christmas Day

Page 25

A 1. head, body, face, nose, mouth, tongue, chest
2. eyes, ears, arms, hands, legs, knees
3. fingers, toes

Page 26

B **Singular Nouns**
1. flower 2. ant
3. song 4. violin
5. crab 6. garden
7. fan 8. egg
Plural Nouns
1. dishes 2. books 3. chairs
4. children 5. foxes 6. stars
7. kites 8. trains

Page 27

C 1. foxes 2. toothbrushes
3. camels 4. clowns
5. glasses 6. dentists
7. trees 8. peaches
9. benches 10. watches

Page 28

D 1. ladies 2. keys
3. toys 4. donkeys
5. babies 6. fairies
7. cherries 8. houseflies
9. puppies 10. boys

Page 29

A **Countable Nouns**
bowl sieve tray teaspoon knife whisk egg wooden spoon
Uncountable Nouns
flour sugar salt baking powder milk butter

Page 30

B **Countable Nouns**
book door zoo shoe cake
flower car nut hen table
Uncountable Nouns
grass oil sand snow money
water air gold milk rain

© 2012 Scholastic Education International (S) Pte Ltd ISBN 978-81-8477-746-8

Page 31

C 1. C 2. UC 3. C 4. C 5. C 6. C 7. UC 8. UC 9. C 10. UC

Page 32

D **Countable Nouns**

tree bird nest sticks
leaves eggs lake boy

Uncountable Nouns

wool mud moss wind help

Page 33

A 1. father 2. grandfather 3. nephew 4. headmaster 5. boyfriend 6. emperor 7. cock/rooster 8. bull 9. lion 10. tiger

Page 34

B 1. mother 2. aunt 3. woman 4. waitress 5. sister 6. daughter 7. princess 8. bride

Page 35

C hen: F rooster: M chick: M/F
kid: M/F billy goat: M nanny goat: F
cow: F bull: M calf: M/F
lion: M cub: M/F lioness: F

Page 36

D

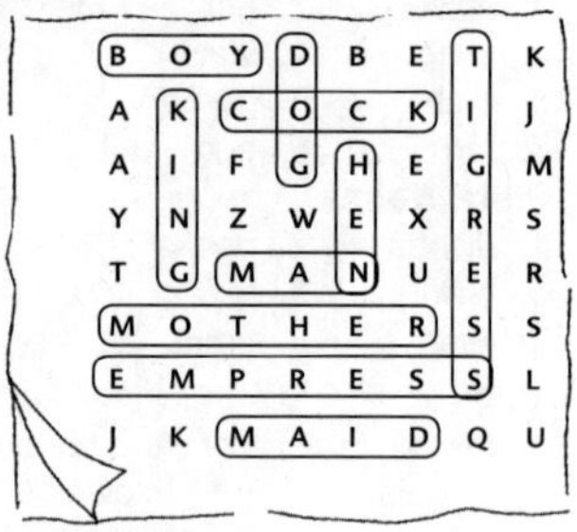

E 1. girl, niece
2. waitress, Queen
3. lioness, cow
4. woman, actress
5. bride, aunt

Page 37

A 1. He 2. She 3. It 4. They

Page 38

B 1. Once upon a time there were three bears. They lived in a cottage in the forest.

First there was Father Bear. He was a great big bear. Then there was Mother Bear. She was a medium-sized bear. And then there was Baby Bear. He was a tiny little bear.

One morning Mother Bear made porridge as usual and poured it into three bowls. But as the porridge was too hot to eat, Mother Bear, Father Bear and Baby Bear left their bowls to cool and went for a walk.

2. the porridge
3. He; She; He; They/It

Page 39

C *Answers will vary—Teacher to check.*

Page 40

D 2. her 3. you 4. me 5. She 6. him 7. you 8. me 9. them 10. they 11. her 12. They 13. them 14. I 15. it 16. I 17. We 18. it 19. you 20. you

Page 41

A 2. That is 3. This is 4. That is 5. This is 6. That is 7. This is 8. That is

Page 42

B 1. these 2. those 3. Those 4. These 5. Those 6. These 7. These 8. Those

Page 43

C 1. these 2. this 3. that 4. those 5. that 6. this 7. these 8. this 9. those 10. this

Page 44

D 1. This 2. that 3. these 4. those 5. This 6. That 7. these 8. those

Page 45

A 1. young 2. colourful 3. interesting 4. everyday 5. simple/clear 6. colour

Page 46

B dirty—6 beautiful—3 strong—2
happy—10 dry—7 old—1
large—9 tall—4 cold—5

Page 47

C 1. young—pretty 2. short—bushy 3. round—square 4. red—colourful 5. empty—glass 6. small—flashy 7. good—brilliant 8. easy—hard 9. clever—smart 10. rainy—sunny

Page 48

D 1. cheerful 2. little 3. large 4. easy 5. wealthy 6. silent 7. hard 8. neat 9. pretty 10. wicked

Page 49

A After a long walk, the three bears returned to their cottage. They were surprised to find someone had been there.

"Somebody has been eating my porridge!" cried Father Bear.

"Somebody has been eating your porridge, too!" Father Bear pointed at Mother Bear's porridge. Mother Bear looked at her porridge.

"Look! Somebody has been eating his porridge!" Father Bear said to Mother Bear, pointing at Baby Bear's porridge.

"Oh! Somebody has been eating our porridge!" the three bears complained.

Page 50

B 1. my 2. your 3. his 4. his 5. her 6. their 7. our 8. its

Page 51

C 1. his 2. their 3. its 4. her 5. your 6. our 7. my 8. her 9. their 10. his

Page 52

D 1. her 2. her 3. my 4. your 5. his 6. our 7. their 8. her

Page 53

A The giant sat down and asked his wife to bring him his hen. She went out and soon came back, carrying a beautiful hen in her arms. She put it on the table in front of the giant. "Lay!" roared the giant and the hen laid an egg.

Jack was peeping from the cupboard. He saw that the egg was made of pure gold. He told himself that if he could have the hen, he and his mother would never be poor again.

Then the giant and his wife ate their dinner. They had so much to eat and drink that they soon fell asleep. Jack quickly took the hen from the table and ran out to the beanstalk as fast as he could. He climbed down the beanstalk with the hen under one arm.

When he reached the bottom, he rushed into his mother's cottage and put the hen on the table. "Lay!" he said. His mother was surprised to see the hen lay a beautiful golden egg.

Jack and his mother became rich and lived happily for many years.

Page 54

B 1. past 2. since 3. at 4. by 5. on 6. for 7. behind 8. near 9. on 10. over 11. into 12. under

Page 55

C 1. She is in the kitchen.
2. It is under the tree / near the tree / next to the tree.
3. She is standing between the trees.
4. It is on the wall / above the sofa.
5. They are playing in the garden / outside the house / in front of the house.
6. They are (flying) over the trees / above the trees / in the air.

© 2012 Scholastic Education International (S) Pte Ltd ISBN 978-81-8477-746-8

Page 56

D 1. at 2. in 3. on 4. in
5. at/in 6. on 7. on 8. at
9. for 10. over 11. at/by 12. in

Page 57

A 1. is 2. am 3. is 4. is
5. is 6. is 7. are 8. is
9. is 10. is

Page 58

B 1. am 2. is 3. is 4. are
5. are 6. is 7. is 8. are
9. is 10. is 11. are 12. am

Page 59

C 2. are not 3. is not
4. are not 5. is not
6. is not 7. is not
8. are not

Page 60

D 2. you're 3. he's 4. she's
5. it's 6. we're 7. they're
8. isn't 9. aren't

Page 61

10. he isn't / he's not
11. she isn't / she's not
12. it isn't / it's not
13. we aren't / we're not
14. they aren't / they're not
15. She's 16. isn't 17. I'm
18. They're 19. isn't 20. aren't

Page 62

A 1. was 2. was 3. were
4. was 5. were 6. was
7. was 8. were 9. was

Page 63

B 1. was 2. was 3. was
4. was 5. was 6. were
7. were 8. was 9. were
10. were

C 1. were 2. was 3. was
4. were 5. were

Page 64

D 1. wasn't 2. wasn't
3. wasn't 4. wasn't
5. weren't 6. weren't
7. weren't 8. wasn't
9. weren't 10. wasn't
11. weren't 12. wasn't
13. wasn't 14. weren't
15. weren't

Page 65

A 1. walk 2. sing
3. answer 4. speak
5. climb 6. play
7. watch 8. go
9. carry 10. keep

Page 66

B 1. can't 2. Can; can
3. Can; can't 4. can't; can
5. can't 6. Can
7. can 8. can
9. can; can't 10. can't

Page 67

C 1. May 2. may
3. may 4. may not
5. may not 6. may
7. may; may not / may not; may
8. may not 9. may
10. May; may not 11. may
12. may not

Page 68

D 1. should; shouldn't 2. shouldn't
3. should 4. shouldn't
5. should 6. should
7. should 8. shouldn't
9. should 10. shouldn't

Page 69

A 1. washes 2. like 3. borrows
4. fit 5. close 6. make
7. takes 8. cross 9. helps
10. live 11. reads 12. goes

Page 70

B The giant panda is a very rare animal.
It lives in the bamboo forests on some mountain slopes in China.

It is as big as a bear and has a white chubby body with black legs. It has a black patch around each eye.

The giant panda feeds only on bamboo shoots, stems and leaves. But the areas where bamboo grows well have become smaller. So the Chinese grow bamboo in special areas for the giant panda to eat.

Page 71

C 1. is 2. build 3. lay
4. are 5. hear 6. live
7. runs 8. cry 9. eat
10. grow 11. make 12. taste

Page 72

D *Answers will vary—Teacher to check.*

Page 73

A 1. There was once a wolf who wanted to kill a sheep for dinner. He found a sheepskin and wrapped it round himself. Then he crept into a field full of sheep and pretended to graze all day just as they did.

When night came, the shepherd rounded the sheep into a pen. He did not know that one of them was really a wolf. The wolf walked round the pen, looking for the fattest sheep to kill.

Unfortunately for him, however, the shepherd came back to the pen to look for a sheep for his dinner. He picked a large one. To his surprise, it was a wolf wearing a sheepskin!

Page 74

B 1. baked 2. hit 3. died
4. saw 5. visited 6. celebrated
7. lost 8. built 9. began
10. changed

Page 75

C 1. watched 2. gave 3. wrote
4. won 5. borrowed 6. climbed
7. washed 8. laughed

Page 76

A Miss Lee told us this morning that our school will stage a play called "Hansel and Gretel" during the school holidays. Miss Lee will direct the play. We shall take part in the play.

Mark will play the role of the woodcutter. Susan will take the part of the stepmother. I shall act Hansel. Kate will be Gretel.

The school will invite all our parents to the play. The play will be fun and everyone will enjoy it.

Page 77

B 1. shall be 2. will start
3. shall take 4. shall go
5. will grow 6. shall leave
7. will hurt 8. Shall...visit
9. Shall...play 10. Will...help
11. will use 12. will paint
13. will have 14. will get
15. will watch

Page 78

C 2. will go for a swim in the pool.
3. will surf the Internet/will work at the computer.
4. will read his storybooks.
5. will play cards with her friends.
6. will make his own kite and fly it.

Page 79

A 1. sweetly 2. neatly 3. quietly
4. safely 5. carefully 6. fairly
7. quickly 8. happily 9. easily
10. softly

Page 80

B 1. outside 2. here 3. there
4. everywhere 5. away 6. over
7. downstairs 8. close

Page 81

C 1. before 2. now 3. soon
4. yesterday 5. tomorrow
6. late 7. early 8. Today
9. first 10. yet

Page 82

D It was almost midnight, but Cinderella did not notice this. She and the prince
were talking cheerfully to each other. Then the clock began to strike. Cinderella quickly stood up and ran out of the ballroom.

© 2012 Scholastic Education International (S) Pte Ltd ISBN 978-81-8477-746-8

As she was running down the steps, Cinderella carelessly dropped one of her glass slippers. But she ran on, hoping anxiously to reach her carriage in time.

When she went near, however, her carriage and horses all disappeared. Hopelessly, Cinderella continued her run home. As she ran, her ball gown changed back into her old ragged dress.

At last she was safely back in her kitchen. She sat down slowly, and thought sadly how her night out had come to an end.

Page 83

A

Amy & May: Mum, can we go outside and play?

Mum: Well, the day is fine but it is windy and cold. Don't go outside or you might catch cold.

May: Please, Mum. We're bored and I've finished my homework.

Mum: Then you could help Dad or Grandma, or you could clean your room.

Amy: We've already offered to help but they said no, and we've cleaned our room.

Mum: Then be sure you get back before three o'clock.

Amy & May: Thanks, Mum!

Page 84

B 1. or 2. and 3. or
4. and 5. but/and

Page 85

C 2. A train is fast but a bus is slow.
3. An ox is strong but a kitten is weak.
4. A giant is tall but an elf is short.
5. An elephant is heavy but a feather is light.

Page 86

A 1. 7 2. 3 3. 7 4. 3
5. 3 6. 3 7. 7 8. 7
9. 3 10. 7

B 1. Uncle Charles bought a poodle.
2. Dave won the first prize for Mathematics.
3. Miss Lee teaches English in a primary school.
4. Dad is enjoying his coffee.

Page 87

5. The children are building a sandcastle.
6. They are eating their dinner.
7. Sue is reading a storybook.
8. I hurt my leg yesterday.
9. Hens lay eggs.
10. Tom is flying his kite.

C 2. (a) An elephant has a long nose.
(b) An elephant is a big and strong animal.
(c) An elephant can help people do work.

Page 88

3. (a) Mum asked us to keep quiet.
(b) Our teacher asked us to keep quiet.
(c) Uncle John asked us to keep quiet.
4. (a) They are waiting for the bus.
(b) Mr and Mrs Ross are waiting for the bus.
(c) The schoolchildren are waiting for the bus.
5. (a) John and his dog are in the garden.
(b) John and his dog like to play in the rain.
(c) John and his dog go to the park every day.

Page 89

D 1. Some birds cannot fly.
2. The dog is barking at the stranger.
3. I am listening to music.
4. Uncle Tom bought Peter a present.
5. This book is very interesting.
6. The police officers are chasing the thief.
7. Dogs and cats often fight.
8. The children are swimming in the pool.
9. These books have lots fo pictures.
10. The weather was very windy yesterday.

Pages 90–94: Revision Test

A 1. an 2. the 3. the
4. a 5. an

B 6. is 7. are 8. am
9. were 10. was

C 11. strong 12. happy 13. dirty
14. noisy 15. lazy

D 16. in 17. between
18. under 19. near 20. on

E 21. you 22. We
23. cherries 24. he
25. calves 26. isn't
27. We 28. that
29. his 30. lived

F 31. (1) 32. (3) 33. (3)
34. (1) 35. (2) 36. (4)
37. (2) 38. (3) 39. (4)
40. (4)

G 41. on 42. are
43. an 44. doesn't
45. he 46. shelves
47. in 48. weeds
49. the 50. of

© 2012 Scholastic Education International (S) Pte Ltd ISBN 978-81-8477-746-8